Going to the Beach

LEVEL 0

DECODABLES BY jump!

Teaching Tips

Lilac Level 0

This book focuses on teaching the earliest readers how to read a book by following images and text from left to right.

Before Reading

- Discuss the title. Ask readers what they think the book will be about.

Read the Book

- Encourage readers to describe what they see on each page.
- Ask questions to help readers understand the story and its progression.
    - What happens at the beginning of the book?
    - What happens at the end of the book?
    - How do we know?

After Reading

- Ask readers what part of the book they liked best. Have them find the page or pages that showed this.
- Have readers imagine a different ending for the book. What else could have happened?

This edition is published by arrangement with Booklife Publishing.

North American adaptations © 2024 Jump!
5357 Penn Avenue South
Minneapolis, MN 55419
www.jumplibrary.com

Decodables by Jump! are published by Jump! Library.

Library of Congress Cataloging-in-Publication Data is available at www.loc.gov or upon request from the publisher.

ISBN: 979-8-88996-756-9 (hardcover)
ISBN: 979-8-88996-757-6 (paperback)
ISBN: 979-8-88996-758-3 (ebook)

Photo Credits

Images are courtesy of Shutterstock.com. With thanks to SuperStock, Getty Images, Thinkstock Photo and iStockphoto.
Cover– XiXinXing. p4–5– TY Lim, Peathegee Inc/Blend Images. p6–7– wavebreakmedia, XiXinXing. p8–9– wavebreakmedia. p10–11– AboutLife, gorillaimages.

About Reading

When we read a book, we go from left to right, like this:

Some books just have pictures, like this:

Some books have words and pictures, like this:

Close the book and flip it over to read The Pet Store!

Close the book and flip it over to read Going to the Beach!

The Pet Store

LEVEL O

DECODABLES BY jump!

Teaching Tips

Lilac Level 0

This book focuses on teaching the earliest readers how to read a book by following images and text from left to right.

Before Reading

- Discuss the title. Ask readers what they think the book will be about.

Read the Book

- Encourage readers to describe what they see on each page.
- Ask questions to help readers understand the story and its progression.
  - What happens at the beginning of the book?
  - What happens at the end of the book?
  - How do we know?

After Reading

- Ask readers what part of the book they liked best. Have them find the page or pages that showed this.
- Have readers imagine a different ending for the book. What else could have happened?

This edition is published by arrangement with Booklife Publishing.

5357 Penn Avenue South
Minneapolis, MN 55419
www.jumplibrary.com

Decodables by Jump! are published by Jump! Library.

Library of Congress Cataloging-in-Publication Data is available at www.loc.gov or upon request from the publisher.

ISBN: 979-8-88996-756-9 (hardcover)
ISBN: 979-8-88996-757-6 (paperback)
ISBN: 979-8-88996-758-3 (ebook)

Photo Credits
Images are courtesy of Shutterstock.com. With thanks to SuperStock, Getty Images, Thinkstock Photo and iStockphoto.
Cover– spectrelabs. p4–5– TY Lim, Peathegee Inc/Blend Images. p6–7– wavebreakmedia, XiXinXing. p8–9– wavebreakmedia. p10–11– AboutLife, gorillaimages.

About Reading

When we read a book, we go from left to right, like this:

Some books just have pictures, like this:

Some books have words and pictures, like this:

Vitakraft
EMOTION
Kracker
Biscuits
3 FOR 2
ROLLI NIS
WHOLESOME

9

L